To Hamish and Sue

A W I N T E R J O U R N E Y

Photographs from around Aberfeldy,
Kenmore and Glen Lyon

James Millar

by James Millar

AN INTRODUCTION

"Always go a little further into the water than you feel you're capable of being in, go a little out of your depth, and when you don't feel that your feet are quite touching the bottom, you're just about in the right place to do something exciting."

David Bowie, 1998

As a professional photographer for over 20 years, I normally work for other people, shooting commissions for performers, covering events, shooting magazine features or architectural photography. So when I decided I wanted to take some time out to do a personal project, I had no expectations of what the photos might become.

The only brief I gave myself was to revisit all those places I'd loved as a child, I'd heard stories about, or which had a personal resonance for me, and try to push myself photographically. I got into the discipline of editing the day's pictures and posting a selection onto my blog. It was wonderful when I realised people were beginning to follow my work. Readers of the blog started to get in touch with encouraging words and suggestions of places to go. The blog led to a meeting with Kevin at the Watermill and this book.

"A-BER-FEL-DY!"

My Granny and Grandpa bought a small cottage on Kenmore Street in Aberfeldy just after the war. If you've ever seen the film *'Withnail and I'* you'll have an idea of the spartan conditions we enjoyed on family holidays, with baths in the kitchen sink, and one open fire 'heating' the whole house. But we still loved it. By the time we had got as far as Dunkeld, my sisters and I would start chanting "A-Ber-Fel-Dy!" still half an hour before we reached the town. It did my parents' heads in.

THE
BIRKS'O'ABERFELDY

I've been walking up the Birks'o'Aberfeldy since I was a toddler. The waterfall
seemed like Niagara Falls to me back then, it was so huge. Scotland's greatest poet,
Robbie Burns, made the Birks famous - and renamed the former Dens of Moness in
the process - when he stopped for a break on his way to the Moness Falls to write a
poem - or possibly to get his breath back.

"Bonie lassie, will ye go,
Will ye go, will ye go,
Bonie lassie, will ye go
To the birks of Aberfeldy!

"Now Simmer blinks on flowery braes,
And o'er the crystal streamlets plays;
Come let us spend the lightsome days,
In the birks of Aberfeldy.

"While o'er their heads the hazels hing,
The little birdies blythely sing,
Or lightly flit on wanton wing,
In the birks of Aberfeldy."

"The braes ascend like lofty wa's,
The foaming stream deep-roaring fa's,
O'erhung wi' fragrant spreading shaws-
The birks of Aberfeldy:

"The hoary cliffs are crown'd wi' flowers,
White o'er the linns the burnie pours,
And rising, weets wi' misty showers
The birks of Aberfeldy:

"Let Fortune's gifts at randoe flee,
They ne'er shall draw a wish frae me;
Supremely blest wi' love and thee,
In the birks of Aberfeldy."

Robert Burns, 1787

ONE WEEK LATER

The temperature rises, the snow
thaws, and Robbie Burns's
favourite gorge shrugs off its
austere, monochromatic overcoat
to reveal its vivid colours.

COMMUNITY BRIDGE
LOGIERAIT

The community-owned bridge at Logierait harks back to the time when the railway cut a swathe through this corner of Perthshire. The trains are gone now, leaving behind ghost cuttings, embankments and bridges.

Opened in 1865 by the Inverness and Perth Junction Railway, Logierait Bridge was another casualty of the Beeching cuts in the 1960s, that saw the closure of over half of the UK's train stations.

In 1964, the last train crossed over this bridge, which then passed into the ownership of the Kinnaird Estate and residents campaigned to save the vital crossing.

In 1994 the bridge was gifted to the Logierait Bridge
Company, who restored and reopened it in 2001. It's the
only community-owned ex-railway bridge in the country.

TOWN SQUARE
ABERFELDY

The arrival of the railway in Aberfeldy in 1865 heralded a new era of prosperity for the town, bringing wealthy visitors and transforming the centre into a modern town square. Aberfeldy station closed in 1965, exactly 100 years later.

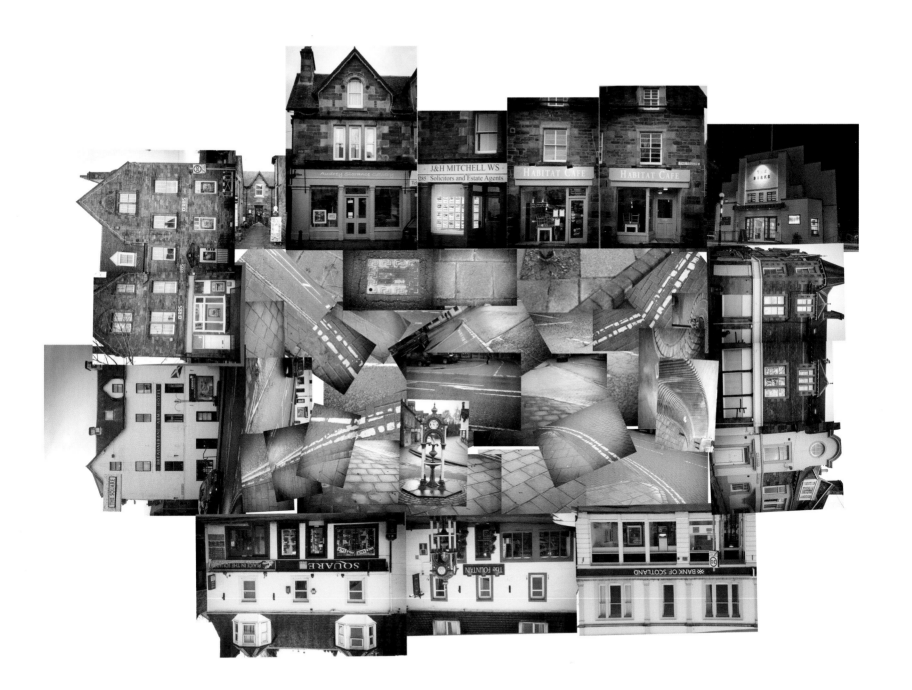

THE BIRKS
CINEMA

As a boy I remember spending my pocket money in Aberfeldy's slightly down-at-heel amusement arcade, before it fell into a state of near dereliction, and finally closed in 2004.

It was a great delight to see the building rise from the ashes and, through an incredible community effort, return to its original 1939 glory, becoming the town's cinema once again.

LOOKING TOWARDS
WEEM WOOD

CREIFF
ROAD

WHITE-OUT ON KENMORE STREET

I hope I never lose the childlike glee of seeing the first flakes of falling snow through the window, and rushing outside to find the street shrouded in a magical white cloak.

OVER 100 YEARS
OF MAKING DRAMS

The railway once led right up to the distillery warehouse doors, and transported Aberfeldy's single malt to whisky lovers far and wide. Although the steam engine stationed outside the distillery no longer leaves the town, Aberfeldy Single Malt certainly does. I recently picked up a bottle in Istanbul Airport.

THE BLACK WATCH INN

I wasn't exactly terrified of the Black Watch, but any pub named after the most feared regiment of World War I, the 'Devils in Skirts' is worth approaching with caution. It's always been a home to some colourful characters. I remember my Dad talking about the rat-catcher who kept a ferret in his pocket.

His habit was to get blind drunk. The pub's landlord would see him off with an "Away home with you, Jimmy".

Then, before the night was out, he'd sober up enough to come back for last orders and maybe also one of the pub's epic 'lock-ins' of days gone by.

ABERFELDY UNDER A BLANKET OF SNOW

A trek up the remnants of General Wade's Road gives a wide view overlooking the town. The road originally ran all the way to Crieff.

GLEN LYON

I've been coming here my whole life, picnicking on the river bank, collecting frogspawn in the rock pools and throwing myself into the old salmon pool, ignoring my family's warnings about the cold. The water always stinging like needles and sucking the air from my lungs.

The longest enclosed glen in Scotland is lonely yet jaw-droppingly beautiful. Once quite densely populated, the Highland Clearances of the 19th century left a only a hundred strong population along the 34 miles between Fortingall and Loch Lyon.

THE ROAD TO BRIDGE OF BALGIE

Towering mountains line the road as
it snakes towards Bridge of Balgie.

THE ROMAN BRIDGE

Halfway along the glen is a packhorse bridge, known locally as the 'Roman Bridge', which crosses a tributary below a waterfall on the south bank of the River Lyon.

How it got its Roman moniker is a bit of a mystery as the bridge is believed to have been built in the 1600s or 1700s.

GLEN LYON POST OFFICE
BY THE BRIDGE OF BALGIE

The Post Office is also a shop and tearoom serving the remote community - and a welcome refuge for walkers on a wet day.

At Bridge of Balgie, the road forks left up towards Ben Lawers and the Tarmachan Ridge. My father's favourite mountain range, it's one of the finest high level ridges in all of Scotland.

Carn Na Marbh
PLAGUE BURIAL SITE, FORTINGALL

On this rock in the middle of a field, there is an inscription. I have to admit it made me recoil slightly, as though I might still get infected:

Here lie the Victims of the
Great Plague of the 14th Century:
Taken here on a Sledge, drawn by a
White Horse, led by an old Woman

Inhabited since the Bronze Age, Fortingall may or may not be the birth place of Pontius Pilate, and may or may not contain the oldest living thing in Europe: but one thing is certain, the yew tree in the churchyard has been there over 5,000 years.

The village that surrounds this ancient yew is more recent than it looks, designed in the 1880s by architect James MacLaren. It was inspired not only by 16th and 17th century Scottish homes, but also by thatched cottages and building features from Devon. His work was an early example of the Arts & Crafts style later embraced by Charles Rennie Mackintosh.

STANDING STONES

Perthshire has as many standing stones as the rest of the United Kingdom put together. The huge stone circles were erected around four thousand years ago, a millennium after the Fortingall yew took seed.

Their use was practical as well as ritualistic; the stone circles charted the sun's movements to mark planting and harvest times for early farmers.

The structures served their communities for thousands of years, evolving into more and more sophisticated seasonal clocks over the millennia, and also marking burial sites.

KENMORE

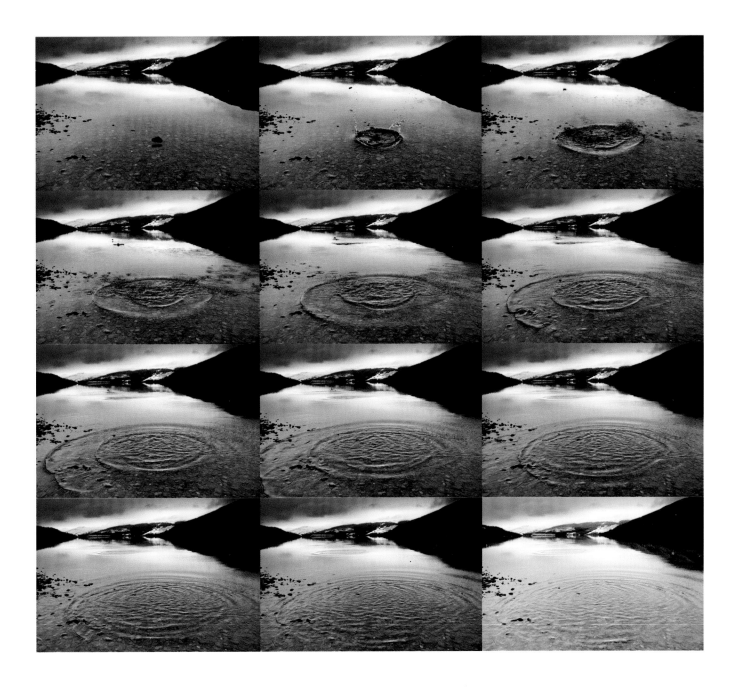

On the banks of a glassy Loch Tay at Acharn, I remember my Dad teaching
me to skim a stone, whilst sausages sizzled on our old camping stove.

THE CRANNOG

From about 600 BC the first residents of Loch Tay lived not by the loch but literally on it. Crannogs were giant round huts on stilts, and once there were eighteen of them in Loch Tay. Some were inhabited until the Middle Ages. You could fit a family of thirty and all their animals inside.

The crannog now standing in Loch Tay is a faithful reconstruction of the originals, based on painstaking underwater archeology.

"THE BURN RAN RED WITH THE BLOOD OF HIS ENEMIES"

Garth Castle is the stuff of nightmares, straight out of a mediaeval horror story. The towering trees get denser as you make your way from the picturesque hamlet of Keltneyburn up the steep winding dirt track. In the half-light, the stone keep comes into view through the twisted oaks lining the banks of the burn.

The view gets even creepier when you hear the story of its fourteenth century former owner, Alexander Stewart, great grandson of Robert the Bruce, and self-styled Earl of Buchan, better known as the Wolf of Badenoch. Local legend has it that he threw his enemies over the battlements of Garth Castle to their deaths on the rocks below.

The most famous misdeed of this rapacious landowner and Justiciar of Scotia was the burning down of Elgin Cathedral. The Bishop of Murray had the audacity to rebuke the Wolf for deserting his wife. He barely escaped the blaze alive.

CASTLE MENZIES

Stronghold of the
Clan Menzies for over
four centuries.

STEREOSCOPIC VIEW FROM THE WALLED GARDEN

TURN TO PAGE 94 TO LEARN HOW TO VIEW STEREOSCOPIC PICTURES.

THE DEATH MASK OF BONNIE PRINCE CHARLIE

Prince Charles Edward Stuart, or Bonnie Prince Charlie, stayed at Castle Menzies in 1746 on his way to the Battle of Culloden.

He never returned to the castle alive, but his death mask looks out from the living room wall.

TAYMOUTH
CASTLE

The building took forty years to complete, and was done in the nick of time to welcome royal visitor Queen Victoria in 1842. John Campbell, 2nd Marquess of Breadalbane, went to great lengths to accommodate the young queen and her consort, installing a lift so she could get to the first floor in her crinolines, and a secret room with a spy hole, so she could listen in on her council of ministers in the library. Campbell hoped to sell the castle to the queen, but Prince Albert's interest in architecture meant they preferred to design their own Scottish home from scratch, at Balmoral, so his efforts to impress were in vain.

The castle has now been partly renovated, but, up until recently, the looming, dormant monster in the valley has been in a state of slow decay, getting incrementally worse every year. It always felt a little like it needed re-awakening, as if the party has just ended and somebody was due to do a clear up and get it ready for the next event, which never came.

Looking down on Taymouth is a brilliant white castle nestled in the forest. Built around 1506, it became the lookout tower for Taymouth Castle in the Marquess's time.

OUT OF MY DEPTH
CARN GORM

There is a line between being tough and being stupid. People die on mountains in Scotland every year, so you are a fool not to respect nature and the environment.

At that moment, I realised I was a long way from anywhere, in a harsh and unforgiving place and I might be out of my depth.

On a fresh, crisp, wintery morning I set off towards beautiful Invervar in Glen Lyon to climb Carn Gorm, a snow-covered mountain in a spectacular range you can see from Aberfeldy. Glen Lyon's beauty took my breath away as I made my way along the winding road, covered in snow and flanked by steep peaks on either side.

Carn Gorm stands west of Aberfeldy in a group of four munros
known as the Carn Mairg Group, or the Glen Lyon Horseshoe.

Last time I climbed this range was a few years back, with my Dad, on a summer's day.

I hadn't reckoned on the burns. What, in summer, were little inconsequential dribbles, were now partially frozen and part gushing streams. Despite taking care I still ended up with wet feet.

HEAVY GOING

My ascent was only slightly blighted by the hydro-electric works going on above the forested approach path. The roar of a JCB was incongruous with the epic beauty of the scene.

I'd underestimated the extra effort required to walk through knee-deep snow, and I'd also underestimated the amount of clothing I'd need to keep me warm.

There was the summit, just ahead of me, dipping in and out of the clouds as the weather went from clear blue skies to more threatening darkness. I had wet feet, and was starting to get cold when I stopped. It was time to call it a day.

HYDRO
WHERE HUMAN MEETS THE LANDSCAPE

An important part of Scottish electricity is generated by hydroelectric power stations. Massive turbines are driven by the weight of water held up in vast reservoirs, generating power which is cabled out to the community via sub stations, like this one near Kinloch Rannoch.

There's a raw, epic, grandeur to the vast man-made lochs like Loch an Daimh.

ON THE ROAD TO RANNOCH

I'd known about Rannoch Station for years: this improbable railway platform right in the middle of Rannoch Moor, on the main line from London - probably one of the most remote railway stations in the UK.

On a snowy morning, I jumped in my inadequate rear-wheel-drive car and wobbled my way along the snow-covered early morning road.

In the nick of time, I pulled into the station car park. Grabbing a camera from the boot, I ran to the footbridge to watch a train pull into the platform, and then, shortly afterwards, snake its way into the distance.

WATER, WATER EVERYWHERE

After a few weeks of snow, there's a slight rise in temperature in my photo story. The landscape changes from monochrome to dreich. Snowflakes become a persistent light drizzle, and the snow turns to slush.

The rivers swell, burst their banks and flood the fields. Dams start to breech, including Gaur Dam. It caught my eye as I drove from Rannoch Station to Aberfeldy. Getting out of the car, the sound of the water spilling over the top of the dam was cacophonous.

Leaving Kinloch Rannoch, I saw the river had burst its banks, and couldn't resist this stereoscopic picture.

A bit further on, my old friend, the majestic Schiehallion, came into view, its pyramidal summit shrouded in the clouds.

I climbed this mountain when I was seven and have summited it numerous times since. It always takes my breath away - an ancient friendly giant.

TURN TO PAGE 94 TO LEARN HOW TO VIEW STEREOSCOPIC PICTURES.

It's a peculiar sight - a small tower incongruously emerging from Loch Rannoch. Eilean nam Faoileag is a crannog made entirely of stones, built on a sand bank base. It used to be much bigger, but in the last 30 years the level of the loch has been raised by about two metres. At some point in the past there was supposed to have been a small prison on the crannog, belonging to the Robertsons of Struan. The present tower is said to be a facsimile of the prison, built by a Baron Granbley in the 19th century.

I decided to climb to the top of Weem Hill to get a view of the flooded valley below, but strayed from the footpath and found myself wandering beside a raging burn, trampling through denser and denser forest. It had a magic feel, with the moss-covered dry-stone walls and white frosted bare branches.

There was only one road out of Aberfeldy one week, and it was not this one.

STAG

On the way down from Loch an Diamh, I felt some eyes upon me. In the forest a stag was staring at me. Unfazed by my presence and still for a critical moment as I raised my camera, luckily with a long lens already attached.

I'm not sure how long we stared at each other, but then he was off, nimbly covering the ground and crossing a burn. He gave me one final look over his shoulder and disappeared into the forest.

THE BLACK WATCH MONUMENT
AND GENERAL WADE'S BRIDGE

Late returning to Aberfeldy one evening when the
snow was falling heavily again. These pictures were
taken with an old polaroid camera. The green cast is
due to the cold weather affecting the film's chemistry.

CAMERAS: NIKON D800 • NIKON D700 • MAMIYA 7 • POLAROID 635 • KODAK LARGE FORMAT • GOPRO

LENSES: SIGMA 10-20MM • NIKON 28MM 1.4 • NIKON 35MM 1.8 • NIKON 50MM 1.4 • SIGMA 85MM 1.4 • NIKON 80-200MM 2.8.

120 ROLL FILM X8 • POLAROID BACK X5 • WETPLATE GEAR AND CHEMISTRY • MANFROTTO TRIPOD • BILLINGHAM BAGS X2

HOW TO VIEW STEREOSCOPIC PICTURES:

Begin by staring at the two pictures allowing your eyes to relax until three images emerge.

Focus on the middle image. Now with some practice you will see the centre picture become three-dimensional.

ACKNOWLEDGEMENTS

Thanks to my editor Heather Tyrrell who has encouraged and inspired me to make this book
and who has turned my ramblings into something people might be able to understand.

Kevin and Jayne at the Watermill Bookshop in Aberfeldy who have made this whole
book possible and been great collaborators and endlessly patient publishers.

Big thanks to graphic designer Diane Warnes, who kindly gave up her time to help me pull it all together.

Ruary Mackenzie Dodds, for his encouragement and whose book *'Aberfeldy - The History of a Highland Community'*,
has been great source material for many of the stories I've mentioned in this book.

My Dad, Lenox Millar, for his highly entertaining but largely spurious stories of the area and its inhabitants.
"Say something with enough confidence and people will believe you" he's always told me.

Published in 2017 by Watermill Books, The Watermill, Mill Street, Aberfeldy, Perthshire, PH15 2BG
www.aberfeldywatermill.com

Copyright © James Millar

British Library Cataloguing-in-Publication Data

A catalogue record for this book is available from the British Library

ISBN 9780995779501

Designed by James Millar

Printed and bound under the supervision of MRM Graphics, Winslow, Buckinghamshire